200
9/04

About the Cover Design for *Brotherhood*

The three figures represent the divine three-in-one and at the same time show unity or brotherhood, as all three are illumined beings. In unity there is strength, and the three are rising out of the pyramid, the strongest physical foundation known. The pyramid also represents Truth. The top point of the pyramid would be about where the head of the center figure is placed. Since the capstone of the great pyramid with its all-seeing eye symbolizes the Christ, God in expression, the eye is placed in the pyramid to reveal it as the symbol of the Great White Brotherhood. The entire pyramid, then, in this case could be just the capstone. The figures, pyramid, and eye all interact with each other in the design to show that in reality it is all one expression; the symbol of brotherhood.

Cover design by Neologic Conceptual Graphics

BROTHERHOOD

An Impersonal Message

BROTHERHOOD

An Impersonal Message

DeVorss & Company
P.O. Box 550
Marina del Rey, California 90294-0550

ISBN: 0-87516-300-9

First Printing, 1927
Seventh Printing, 1989

Printed in the United States of America

CONTENTS

THE VOICE

YOU who have reached that stage in your climb to the heights where you are no longer seeking anything of self, having tasted of all that the outer world and its human teachers can offer, and something within is strongly insisting that you begin to prove and demonstrate what you have learned by living it and using it to help others who are still seeking;

You, who have felt within the heart a definite call to service and yearn to follow and obey, but who from obeying many urges in the past, only to be disappointed and disillusioned each time by failure of the leaders to be worthy of the Causes they represent, and you are therefore uncertain about this call, and are fearful of not knowing just what you ought to and can do;

You who have not yet had this experience, but who are moved by a strong loving desire to help lift the load from those less fortunately situated, and who would know what is that insistent something within, and whose the voice that thus calls;

Know, one and all, what you feel is My Love quickening into conscious active life in your heart, and what you hear is My Voice calling you to make ready for the Work I have been preparing you for—a Work that is your Work, long waiting for you to do,—when you have proven that self is no longer in control, and that you are willing to let Me lead the remainder of the way.

You who think you are now ready, and

sincerely wish to follow, hear this My Word and seek prayerfully to know My full meaning.

First, remember who I am, I who am in all men, Who am That which speaks through all men, Who am the Self of you who read, dwelling deep within the heart—the innermost of you, and Who seek to come forth as the Christ and to show *Myself*—your Highest Self—to all men.

Remember that I always speak from out the heart, and not from the head, the intellect being but My servant, My interpreter. But when the servant acknowledges not his Master, having grown proud, and deems himself above his station and tries to impress others with his knowledge and importance, then you may know why it is so hard to hear *My* voice and to know when it is I speaking, and why you become so often confused and so uncertain what to do. Therefore it is most necessary that you determine whence comes the voice or voices that so confuse and disturb you.

But, you say, suppose you have not yet reached the stage where you are able actually to hear a voice speaking within and to know it as one assuming to teach or lead you.

Know that it is not an actual voice such as your physical ears hear that speaks; for are not every desire, every urge, every hope, longing, fear, discouragement, anxiety, regret, voices heard just as surely and effectively as audible voices?

And while all such are voices I use to teach you the right from the wrong way, yet My Voice, that you long so to hear and to be always sure is Mine, you will never truly hear and know until you let Love abide and rule in your heart. For Love alone can clear away that in your heart and consciousness which causes you to listen to the voice of self, thus preventing your hearing Me when I speak.

But know, My Child, there are sure ways of knowing when the voice of self speaks, and when I speak—to him who sincerely wills to know, and who is ready to face self, and see and know it for just what it is, and just what it pretends to be and is not.

Self is always in an attitude of fighting for and protecting its own, always afraid of losing something it possesses; and so its voices of criticism, condemnation, anxiety, fear, worry, selfishness, greed, envy, jealousy are ever heard in their efforts to hold your attention; while My Voice of Love and Faith, Hope and Trust, Understanding and

Discrimination always seeks to enlist your interest in the Truth I would unfold to you.

The voice of self is always asking, demanding something for self, is always concerned solely with self. My Voice always points you to and concerns you with others whom I want you to think of and to help.

The voice of self sounds from without, always relates to something in the outer world, or to conditions springing from it. My Voice always sounds from within, relating to things of the Soul-state, your Soul, or your brother's.

The voice of self ever seeks by much reasoning and argument to oppose anything that would deprive the self of some power or prerogative long held or exercised by it. My Voice speaks from deep within the heart and declares the Truth so definitely that unless self has complete control, the mind cannot but accept and recognize it as Truth.

The voice of self is always trying to get from others that which will benefit self, often hiding such benefit behind sophistries put forth to fool the mind into believing they are for others' good. My Voice definitely requires that you denounce the ways of self, that you realize now and always that My Way is just the opposite of that of self; for it is ever the way of loving service to others, instead of getting for self.

Especially would I have you know that any voice that holds out to you any way of gaining knowledge or power at a price other than through earnest seeking first My Kingdom and living the life of My Son is the voice of self, no matter if spoken by those proclaimed to be great teachers, swamis,

yogis, initiates, or masters, and no matter
how much they charge for their teachings.
For the Way unto Me cannot be found except as My Son Jesus taught and lived—the
Way of loving service to others and the
crucifixion of self.

Many have thought they heard My Voice
spoken by such teachers, only to learn what
my real Voice finally making itself heard in
the heart clearly pointed out—that self both
within the teachers and within themselves
cared nothing for Me, but only for what it
could gain for self, and that it was only
head knowledge that was being taught, and
that it contained no spiritual life, and hence
no real power came with it.

Finally, you can always tell when it is *not*
My Voice that speaks; for whenever anything is said that is not wholly good, that is
not spoken in love, that is not as you know

God would say and inspire it, then you may know it is self, trying to keep your mind "separate" so it cannot hear My Voice when I would lead it back to the consciousness of Me.

THE CALL TO SERVICE

WHEN a message comes containing an opportunity for real service, and disclosing a real plan and a real work for the helping of your brothers; not some vague high-sounding ideal, but a definite practical work that your Soul recognizes, and your heart leaps toward in glad response—know that such response is My Voice calling you to the Work I have been preparing you for, and you need not question or doubt, for your Soul commands you to obey.

But if there is no glad response in your heart, not even a faint voice there calling upon you to investigate as there may be something in this for you—and instead there is only a coldness and an entire lack of in-

terest—know that message is for others and
that particular Work is not for you, for you
could be of no assistance, not being ready
for such Work—as yet.

But if hearing, and at first thus happily
responding, if but for a moment, before
doubts crowd in and from outer sources
come advice and argument, criticism of that
particular work or of the way it came to
you, or of the messenger who brought it,
fast smothering the urge in the heart still
trying to hold your attention, know that I
am but trying and testing you, to see if you
are as yet ready for the Work which I always have awaiting My proven and faithful
servants; to see if I can use you to awaken
and prepare my other children so I can unfold My nature in them that they can feel
Me as the Love in their hearts, and can
thereby hear My voice there, and know I

am their Higher and Real Self and that I am calling them also, anxious to lead them forth into the New Day.

While all calls are My Call, each with its separate appeal, yet each is but leading you on to a realization that all outer things that appeal, all calls of ambition, of riches, of leadership, of power, of human love, yea even of Spiritual attainment, are but the allurements of the separate self, that I use to build Me a strong personality in you, with its power of concentration and ability to accomplish; an instrument I thus develop and prepare for use in the fulfillment of My Plan and Purpose. Then when all is ready, in order that there may be nothing to interfere with or hinder Me in such use, one by one I take from you all outer things that still allure, until there is nothing anymore left, nothing and no one you can look or turn to but Me,—and you have learned to want and to know Me as the one and only thing of importance, and the perfect serving of Me becomes the sole concern and ambition of your life.

It is then only I can send you the Great Call and you can hear it *in your heart,* which now has been opened wide for My use alone, and has been cleansed of all desires of self. Then only can you hear that Call, the call to My blessed ones, those who have dedicated themselves to Me and now live only to serve Me in their brothers.

To all such of you, for there are many whom I have so prepared and who have responded, and who are working selflessly as one with Me, I now send the Call to Service, the call to join the Great Brotherhood of Servers; and those who hear and who know My voice and who gladly have learned to heed it, I am opening their eyes and permitting them a vision of My Plan and of My Purpose for the New Age you are now entering, and am enabling them to comprehend the true and glorious meaning of Brotherhood, that Brotherhood I intend soon to bring forth from the Kingdom within, into actual manifestation in men's midst.

Those of you who refuse to align yourselves with others, thinking that unnecessary for you can come to Me direct, and get all the guidance and help you need,—know you are still thinking of self and are not yet ready for true Service. To you I say the days of seeking and getting for self are past— never to return. No more studying to attain powers will I allow. The training period I allotted for such purpose is over. If you but know it, you brought all the "powers" you seek along with you. And I have been trying to teach you in the school of life's experiences and under those I appointed for your discipline and training, that when you are ready to use these powers—which in reality are not yours but Mine—no longer for selfish purposes, but wholly in My Service, I will uncover them to your consciousness and direct you perfectly in their use.

For the Force I formerly gave to man for the growth and development of self is now withdrawn. Henceforth all My Wisdom, Love and Power is poured into and through the Great Brotherhood of the Spirit. He who would receive must go within his heart and find Me as the Christ, His Higher Self, abiding there, and must give up all of personal self and follow Him, must enlist and serve under His banner — the banner of Brotherhood.

It is true you can still come to Me and

get the guidance you need, but only for the use and helping of your fellowmen. No more will I give of My Force to develop the consciousness of the separate self. Now all must go to the use of the Christ—to the binding and lifting of all self-consciousness into the consciousness of Brotherhood.

I now call upon you to *live* and *use* what you so long have been studying and believing with your intellect about Service and Brotherhood. When you believe in your heart, which belief can only come from USE and DEMONSTRATION, then you will truly *BE* and *KNOW* a *Brother,* and not before.

Only you who forget and are no longer concerned with your Soul's status can truly serve Me in your brothers, for when you learn to love your brothers more than self, then you will hear My Voice speaking in your heart telling you what to do and how to do it.

Those who do not want to acknowledge any leader other than their Higher Self and therefore fear to join others in service in outer organizations, thinking such cannot be impersonally or spiritually directed by any human personality,—know that you are indeed striving to obey the voice of your Soul, but ignorantly; for your Soul will never require you to acknowledge or obey any leader who would ask you to do anything to which your Higher Self would not assent. Any such command or requirement of such a leader would immediately absolve you from allegiance in any such organization. But Wisdom also would first require you fully to satisfy your mind as to your Soul's desire, as previously explained, regarding the Call to such Service. For can

you not realize, that all that has gone
before, My bringing you through so
many disappointments and disillusionments,
through all the various experiences and
teachings into a consciousness of Me, as
your Higher and only Self, has been but to
lead you into that wider and deeper consciousness of Me as *the Higher Self also of
your brother,* and that you and your brother thus *become one in Me,* and that *there
is and can be no separation.* That is the true
vision of Brotherhood. When you have
caught that, then you have entered the
Kingdom of My Consciousness and see and
know as I would have you see and know.

Therefore there cannot possibly be any
separation between those consecrated to the
Vision,—all are one, whether in the Spirit
or in the flesh,—they are a part of that
Great White Brotherhood of Spirit, the

most perfect organization that is, for It is Eternal, always was, and always will be; and It is gradually drawing to Itself—one by one — all who have learned and conquered the illusion of self and separation.

Do you want to be separate any more, My children, now that you know the Truth? No, for from now on the great hunger of your life will be for *conscious* union with your Brothers; for only then will you find and truly and fully know Me.

As to any outer organization representing My Kingdom of the Spirit down in the midst of men being directed by a human personality, know that only through human instruments can My Will be done on earth. Even as I can accomplish My Will in large ways by inspiring many minds with My Love through My Spirit—the Christ— within them, so do I inspire many to look only within to Him for leadership,—so that they may realize that He in them and He in everyone of their brothers is One — is I, their True and Only Self. Therefore it is not the personality of such leader they see any more, but only the Master—the Christ —of such personality through whom I work.

Many have thus become His proven and faithful Disciples, My Beloved Sons, and they gladly obey His commands, knowing Him only as their Higher Self, and living only to help others also thus to learn to know and to obey Him; and they, through such selfless love and consequent oneness of purpose as His followers, thus become banded in Spirit in a great army of workers for Him. And all who can similarly learn to follow and serve Him, automatically become one of this invisible army, all under His leadership, and of course guided and directed by His more tested and proven ones — your elder Brothers — My generals and lieutenants, in mundane army terms. And how may you know your elder Brothers, those I have chosen to lead and guide My children into the New Day? By one way only — by that most sure way — by their fruits, by compelling others by their lives and their achievements to recognize the Christ of them.

As in the past they have not been called from the high places, but I have called again the fishers of men—those whose lives are consecrated to the uplifting and helping of their fellows — particularly those who have not sought for self, but only to serve the Christ in their brothers, those whose names are unknown to the outer world for the work they have done, but who have brought thousands and thousands into the consciousness of Me in their hearts, each in his own way.

Think you I can work My will otherwise? It is only through such chosen ones—they who have given themselves over wholly to Me — that I can do My Will upon the earth as I purpose it to be done. To such I give a glimpse of My Plan and My purpose. But think not I work only through such conscious channels. Am I not working My Will through you, and through every one who at any time seeks to obey his Highest Self? Such, in very truth, form My Army —My workers, My servers, My fighters for Truth and Righteousness.

The armies now being used for destruction and to obey the will of human kings or rulers are but man's using My Heavenly plan of organization for his selfish and inhuman purposes.

But the day of such use of My Heavenly plan is soon over. The Battle of Armageddon soon to be fought on earth will forever drive from men's minds the desire and ability to use My spiritual knowledge and power for other than the benefit and blessing of their fellowmen.

Brotherhood is to be an actual conscious realization of the men of earth, and I call upon you, My children, to help Me and your Brothers of the Spirit to make it so. My Message of Brotherhood is now being broadcast over the whole world. There are many who have caught it from the inner planes and are giving it forth as I have permitted and am enabling them to do, but there is One whom I have chosen and appointed, have made responsible for and given the power to link and to bind all Souls who have found Me into one great army of Servers, consecrated to the work of preparing the Way for the ushering in of the New Day. By his Words and by his Work ye may know him. Make no mistake, but seek him the spirit of whose words and deeds is that your Highest Self approves and glorifies.

A VOICE CRYING IN THE
WILDERNESS

TRY, My children, to realize Brotherhood
is a REALITY, that it is not merely what
ordinary minds think is only an ideal. For
a real and very potent and actual Brotherhood exists, as many are having proven to
them these days, those who have felt My
Love in their hearts and are following Its
leadings, which in very truth is My Voice
speaking, the Voice of My Spirit — the
Christ—abiding in the hearts of all men.

For in unaccountable yet unmistakable
ways have I brought some of you who read
into contact with individuals whom you feel
are Brothers, though you may never have
met them before—in the outer. And again

have I brought to you, or have led you to
those who needed the very help which seemingly only you could give; the surest evidence being your surprise at hearing yourself say words and feel a great love within
you pushing them forth, which you had no
forethought of saying, and which proved
to be just the words those others afterwards
claimed they had come to you to hear.

Who led or sent such to you? Who were
so well acquainted with both you and them
that They knew beforehand just what you
would say and what those others needed?
Who but They in the Spirit, My Ministers,
Who were so at one with you because of the
love They bore Me in you and in them that
They could inspire you to say what you did?
Constantly perhaps are some of you made
aware of such service you are called upon
to render, and likewise are you made to feel

in some undefinable but very actual way that you are related not only to those whom thus you are led to help, but as well to those invisible Ones in Spirit Who brought such to you for such help.

All must admit there is a Brotherhood of the Spirit, and that such is an invisible Brotherhood in no way related to the flesh. Can you doubt that Jesus and His Disciples, Paul, Elijah, and the other great prophets; Moses, Jacob, Abraham, of the Old Testament; and all the other Just Men Made Perfect of their days and before, as well as those of the many generations since, who have followed the Christ, have mastered self and have learned to live His life,—can you not see that They are of that Brotherhood?

If not, where are They now and what are They doing? Surely They are living in the Kingdom I prepared for such, and are working — serving there, are They not? Working and serving in Spirit, striving to inspire and lead Their younger brothers still in the flesh consciousness to a like knowledge with Theirs of the Christ within their own hearts, and to follow Him unto the Resurrection and into Eternal Life — their Divine Heritage, and where these perfected Souls are now dwelling, even though they may be living in bodies that are walking upon the earth.

What else can be the goal of our humanity, and can you imagine anyone who has come into the Christ Consciousness ceasing thus to serve, no matter if he be in the Kingdom of the Spirit or in the flesh, until all his brothers have come into possession of the same fruits of the Spirit he is enjoying?

True Brotherhood is of the heart and

seeks only to lift up and love and bless, even though the weaknesses and limitations of the lower self stand forth glaringly. He who can look through these and see only Me, the Higher Self of his brother, and who proceeds to serve Me, knows the pure joy of My Love and the real meaning of Brotherhood.

Oh, My children, ever refuse to see the personality of your brotherhood, no matter what is said about it, for always I would have you know the Soul shining back of the mask. If you will but wait upon Me within I will let you see through My eyes of Love the sorrowful one yearning for recognition there, and who at your kind words of understanding will respond in such unmistakable way you will surely learn the truth of My words.

Open your heart and let Love out, and

you will not only soon feel Me big within you, but you will learn what Brotherhood truly is; for REAL Brothers will come into your life and prove a source of wondrous joy and great blessing to you.

HE WHO IS TO COME

A S ALL MEN deep in their hearts would deem it an inestimable privilege to be able to see the Lord Jesus Christ face to face, and to commune with Him, if they thought such were possible, — know, you who earnestly seek for such privilege, that such is not only possible, but the Master waits yearningly for that very thing, and is in very truth the inspirer of that desire in your heart, trying to tell you that He is ever abiding in the Kingdom within you, guiding and teaching and preparing you through one of His disciples, who has become sufficiently one in consciousness with Him, for that day.

For even as He taught when on earth,

that He, the Christ in all men, is the Way, the Truth and the Life, and no man can come unto Me except through finding and knowing Him within his own heart, so have He and all of His many disciples ever since been helping man to find the Christ within themselves, so they also can come unto Me.

For the Christ of Him and the Christ of you is One—is My Spirit in man, the Image and Likeness of Me in which I conceived Man in the beginning; and it is Jesus Christ —that Image and Likeness—that Ideal— that is the Light and the Life in all men that, out of the darkness of self, is pushing forth and growing them until My Word fully becomes flesh.

All who are manifesting in physical bodies today are not here by accident or because of some whim of fate, but are here either because they chose to be here at this par-

ticular time, to help their Brothers prepare
for the ushering in of the New Day, having
dedicated themselves to that Service ages
ago in a past life, or because I brought them
the opportunity of redeeming through present service the errors of the past—the long-
past. To all men this present time is the
chance of adjustment, not of one life, but
of many—the accounting of an Age, if they
will listen to and hear My Voice speaking
in their hearts, and will seek only to serve
Me.

Therefore, My children, turn within
where I abide and try earnestly to hear and
know My Voice speaking in your heart.
Turn from the voices of self whose mouth-
piece is the intellect, and who would bind
you longer to the world of the senses by
leading you to believe their false reports.
Think earnestly and well, for you have at

this time the opportunity of many, many lives. Serve Me henceforth in your brothers; espouse with a whole heart the Cause of **HIM WHO IS TO COME.** Stand shoulder to shoulder with your fellows who have enlisted and are training for the Great Battle for Righteousness, and I promise you will have the supreme joy and privilege of meeting and communing with Him face to face, and of seeing Him rule in a purified and regenerated world.

LEADERS

YOU, My chosen ones, whom I have called in the past to gather My little ones that I might awaken them from the sleep of self and separateness and teach them through you the way unto Me,—know that you have been faithful and many have come unto Me through you, and through this Service have I drawn you and them close to Me in preparation for the Greater Day and for the far greater Service that awaits.

For you must know that I had a purpose in choosing you for such Work and in drawing such unto Me, and that as you and they realize this and look forward to the utter forgetting and losing of self will I have in you pure and empty hearts in which I can live My life, do My Will and be My Self on earth, even as in Heaven.

But, Alas! Some of you seem to have forgotten that you are My Ministers and you have been doing this all for Me, and, from long being looked up to as shepherds of these My children and from being followed by many such whom you have allowed to lean upon you, and for this privilege have encouraged them to provide for your physical support and comfort, as a consequence you have grown to believe such are specially attached to you and should look no further, as *you* are able to feed their hunger for knowledge and to care for all their Spiritual needs.

I know that those to whom this applies may not have realized this, but I ask you now to search deep within and see if it is partly, if not wholly, true; that when some of your followers come to you with a teaching from a different source, or especially from some new messenger I have sent forth whose appeal is drawing many to hear him or her, you are sure you have so conquered personality that no words of criticism either of the messenger or of his message are voiced by you, but only kind and loving expressions of a true Brother, a pointing out so clearly that the other messenger is a most dear Brother—another of My beloved sons sent to do My bidding; so that your hearers will go away uplifted and inspired with a high spirit of understanding and will praise God for the new realization of Brotherhood that has come to them.

If you have caught this Vision you are truly blessed and you remain My chosen one for the greater Service, but to all others I now declare the day of separate Movements

and separate teaching is past, for all such
have been but the way and the means I
have used to prepare and fit those of My
former servants whom I sent into earth life
to lead My children into the New Day,
when My Kingdom is to be brought down
upon earth even as it is in Heaven, and
when there will be only one Movement and
one Church, the Church of the LIVING
Christ.

To those so called do I now give the task
of awakening their Brothers, of calling them
unto repentance, of pointing out the One
and Only way, *THE WAY OF THE
HEART,* which is the straight and narrow
path that leads to the gate which admits
the Servants and Warriors gathering to
serve under *HIM WHO IS TO COME.*

You who up to the present have been un-
willing to consider actively aligning your

movement with others, thinking you have been receiving direct from Me or from one of My sons in the Spirit all the guidance needed to lead you and your followers into the Light of the New Day, and that you can hold them and guide them up the slippery path that leads to self-mastery by means of such inspiration, which has proved so helpful in the past,—know that I now call you to join with your Brothers who have already responded to My Call and who have enlisted in that Eternal Army called Brotherhood, which must include all who would enter and participate in the Kingdom of Love and Righteousness, that I purpose soon to establish on earth.

The work you have been doing in the past is practically finished—as far as you can go with it; that has largely been concerned with the head—an awakening of the understanding and a quickening of the higher faculties of the intellect of those you have been teaching; but now the time is come when all such must be put to the real *USE* for which they have been developed. If you have taught them impersonally and have led them thereby to understand clearly that all self-development was for the later use of the Higher Self under the direction of the Christ, then you will not doubt or hesitate, but you and all your true followers will know that this is the Call for which you have been preparing them, and for which you have long been waiting.

But if you are listening to the voice of self and to its subtle pointing out that by joining with others you will lose prestige, and your followers will become enamored with other teachings, and what more vitally concerns you, you may lose the income they are now providing for your support and sustenance,—to you I bring the supreme test —that of deciding this day whom you shall serve—God or Mammon.

Make no mistake—no longer can you deceive yourself. Those who truly love Me must give up *ALL* and follow Me. The Lord Christ calls; He will have no half-hearted or weak-kneed servants. All those who belong in the Great White Brotherhood must absolutely and finally renounce self and all its claims, and must now live only to Serve. In such the separate self exists no more, for they see the One Self in all men —and have learned the glorious meaning or Brotherhood; — they have truly found Me, and that I in them and I in their brother am the *ONE* and *ONLY SELF*.

But there are still many fine and earnest teachers who have become so wrapped up in their own vision and mission, which I inspired in them in the past, and are so concerned about fulfilling that mission that they cannot feel any real sympathy with others having an equal or greater vision. In fact they will not take the trouble to investigate or even read carefully what others are doing, and therefore cannot speak or advise intelligently with their followers when questioned about them. These do not realize that this is but a subtle and insidious form of Spiritual selfishness and that it is preventing their comprehending the full meaning of Brotherhood, and therefore the real inner meaning of their own Mission; and as a result they are feeding their followers with only the husks of Truth—with but intellectual concepts, no matter how high sounding and beauiful, but which are incapable of inspiring them with the true Spirit of Service and thereby accomplishing what I sent them forth to do — prepare their followers for full participation in the Work of My Holy Brotherhood.

Those teachers and leaders who are so engrossed in what they consider their own Work, as well as those who cannot and will not yield to the call of their Higher Self, will find that one by one their followers will fall away; for many of these followers have likewise heard My Call to Service and no claims of loyalty to a personal leader or Movement can long hold them with My Voice calling in their hearts.

Your work as a leader of a *separate* Movement is finished, for the hearts of all true followers of the Christ hear the cry of Brotherhood, and if you, their leader, do not obey that Call, your followers will and must; for it is that true part of your teaching—your showing them the way unto Me and telling them how they may know My Voice, that first attached them to you. But fear not, if you truly exemplify to your followers that which you have taught, and if you now manifest the Spirit of Real Brotherhood you will find the children I have entrusted to your care will not leave you, but many blessings now to you inconceivable will be added in marvelous ways.

Oh, beloved, can you not see that all your work in the past has been but a preparation for this far greater Work—that of making Brotherhood an actual reality among men? You have been awakening My children, training and unfolding their consciousness so that they could find and know the Christ within,—their True Self, and their only Real Teacher, and so thereby they could enter into My Consciousness and see the illusoriness and falsity of all outer things.

By finding the Christ, they find the Kingdom, and in the Kingdom they learn to
practice *real* Brotherhood. Now you must
help them to make that Brotherhood a *living* Reality. Your work is not finished —
your real work is but just beginning—if you
enlist in that part of the Great White Brotherhood I am forming here on Earth, and to
which I am calling not only you and all My
children who are in your care, but all My
other Ministers and My children in their
care; for the glorious campaign for Righteousness is already started and this time
will be won by My Army whose members
are legion and whose might is supreme. For
remember I Am in them and I am surrounding and protecting them with My
LOVE, and *those* who are with *Me* are far
greater than those who are against me.

EVIL

YOU who are troubled by the problem of evil, thinking that evil is only an illusion, and by recognizing and trying to fight it only gives to it a power over you which otherwise it would not have,—know the truth.

Evil does exist, but only in man's mind, created by his own evil thinking, and it is a very tangible power there—so long as he continues to feed and vitalize it by entertaining such thoughts and allowing them to influence or control his speech and actions.

However, there is a center within man, deep within his heart, where I, the Christ of him abide. *There,* he becomes a center of and one with My Consciousness—his true home, where all is Peace, Purity, Power and Perfection. Whenever man stays outside that home center, no matter if in the world of thought, the world of feeling and desire, or the outermost world of matter, unless his attention is firmly fixed upon Me in that center, or he *knows* his oneness with Me there, all becomes confused and distorted and all tends to distract and separate man's consciousness from Mine and to involve and hold him in these worlds which long ages ago, when he had wholly forgotten Me and imagined himself alone and separate from My Life and My Love, he had created by mentally building them one by one around him, until they grew into definite beliefs, and the outermost became so crystalized a concept that he saw all things in this realm as separate materialized forms, and thought them unquestionably solid and tangible.

And having lost the consciousness of Me and of My Love, and with it the ability to know the Good, the True, and the Perfect of all things, in the darkness of separation in which he now wandered he saw only the shadows of the Real, and these distorted and twisted; and he blasphemed when in his imperfect sight he stumbled in judgment and fell, or was hurt by bumping against unseen obstacles. And thus man conceived and built Evil into the worlds of his consciousness and made of it a power he ever since has thought he must fight, if he would be free of and unhurt by it.

But you who read may see if you will, through the eyes of My Love, that evil exists not where I am, in the Kingdom of My Consciousness,—that center deep within the heart of every man. It exists only without, in that consciousness of separation, — mental, desire or physical worlds, where, if man allows his deeper interest to wander, he becomes enamored with the illusions and error concepts created there back through the ages by millions of other minds similarly deluded.

Evil exists in greater or less degree in all realms of consciousness that man thinks are separate from My Consciousness. But you know where I Am, *God IS*—and *all* in His Kigdom must be and is Good and True, Pure and Holy, Happy and Perfect.

All you need do, therefore, to be free from evil, sin, disease, lack or imperfection of any kind, is to withdraw within to that center, your Real Home, where I AM, and where you will see and know Truth as your own, even as I see and know it. Each man can prove this for himself, but each must come within where I AM to prove it. The way unto Me is open to all, but the way is *through the heart,* treading the path of Love and of Selfless Service.

In that Home Center you can truly say I *AM,* and know WHO *you* are, but the moment you let your interest and attention wander into the outer worlds of the senses and to any of the things within them, you are, as it were, pulled from your center, deluded into a sense of separation, and sucked into an outer and lower plane of consciousness away from God and Good, and you become *involved* in and are seemingly a part of that realm of consciousness where you allowed your interest and attention to become focused for the time being.

But here is the secret by which you can regain your power,—you need only to remember *Who you are,* that your home is back in the center, in the Kingdom there

where I AM—where the God of you IS;
and then to re-focus your attention and interest there by *seeing* and *feeling* yourself
centered therein and surrounded by and
filled with *My Love,*—when *you will actually and truly be there.*

Then by practicing staying in that Love
Center, realizing Who you are—your identi-
ty with Me, and feeling My Love pouring
out through you, as a heart center, you will
find you can look out through and go in
and out of these outer realms of consciousness at will, seeing and knowing they are all
illusions—reflections rather—of the glorious
Realities within the Kingdom, created out
of the substance of those imagined worlds
that exist only by reason of your fancying
them real and separate from My Consciousness; distorted concepts fashioned in ignorance and from efforts to understand their

peculiar influence upon the relation to you.

This is a great secret indeed, and it is waiting for all to know who have found the Way of Love, through the heart, unto Me. For I, God, *AM* Love, and the more you love—the more you forget self—the more do you let Me have *My* way in you. Therefore let My Love, which is My Creative Life flow freely through you. For in very truth you are My agent, My channel of expression; and only through you, whom I created in My Image and Likeness for such purpose, can I pour forth the fullness of My Life and express My Real Self. In fact, I can do nothing outwardly except through you.

Know that the very nature of My Life is to love and bless, to grow and unfold, to heal and make perfect. It will do this naturally and always, if not interfered with by man's wrong thoughts, or by man's ignorant thoughts—his not knowing the mighty power he is wielding by forming thought pictures in his mind, into every one of which My Life flows and vitalizes and outmanifests them, according to the kind of feeling he puts into them.

This accounts for the many inharmonious, troublous and obnoxious conditions now manifesting in your life. But it is just as easy to bring into manifestation the conditions and things you want, as those you do not want; for My Life is ever seeking—rushing, as air into a vacuum—to fill full and outmanifest all your thoughts, especially those into which you put intense feeling; for note carefully this great truth—*feeling* of any kind *is LIFE*, is *My Life* that you use to *vitalize* your thoughts. According to the intensity and quality of feeling—of love or hate, faith or fear, trust or worry, confidence or doubt—you put into your thoughts will they prove a blessing or an evil to you.

This explains how each man—and no one else—is responsible and accountable for all the conditions surrounding him; for remember they exist primarily in his mind as the thought forms he has built there. Therefore, by replacing the pictures there you do not like with those you do like, and focusing your heart's interest and attention upon them, you change the conditions outwardly. When you can once realize that what is manifesting in your outer life — in your body, home, business, world—is only what you are *seeing and holding in your consciousness,* you will begin to clean out your mental house and to build and keep there only the things that will bring you soul satisfaction and happiness.

It also explains how you can help and bless others who are in trouble and unable to help themselves. You, who are abiding in your center of Consciousness where I am, can send My Healing Life to any other center of My Consciousness to the Higher Self of a brother who is sick or weak and knows not in his brain consciousness of My Life within him. By simply opening your heart and letting My Love pour out you can send it direct to him; for in My Consciousness there is no space or time separation, and to Me you and your Brother are one with and part of Me. Just realize—*feel* and *see* My Love flow from you to him, who is in very truth your Self, because he is My Self; *see* It pouring forth from deep *within,* surrounding and filling him—just as it pours forth from *within you*—as a Radiant White Energizing Force—that spiritual Life Force which grows and fructifies and heals all living things. See it flowing from deep within his heart and radiating outward, through his mental, emotional and physical consciousness and bodies, permeating and flooding every part of them, and then surrounding and enclosing them in pure, brilliant, White Light—the Light of My Holy Love, which no evil or inharmony or imperfection can touch or come near, no more than darkness can be where there is brilliant light.

Just to the extent that you actually KNOW this and can perfectly visualize and *see* it taking place, and can *feel* my tender love inspiring, flooding and uniting the consciousness of you both, will a perfect healing take place, and Evil and all its minions will be driven back into the darkness of nothingness and ignorance whence they came. For in very truth will it be My Life that is rushing into and which will vitalize the new and true concept thus formed in your minds and hearts, and which will make it a REALITY. For then the without will have become as the within, and you will see with the Light of My Love that *all* consciousness is My Consciousness.

The KNOWING of this Truth will make you and all who are concerned about the problems of Evil, Disease, Lack or Imperfection, FREE.

Do not pass by this article with just one reading, but go over it again and again, meditating earnestly upon every sentence and phrase, until you have made all the great Truth hidden back of the words *your own*. If you do this you will find you will be able shortly to demonstrate this Truth by thus blessing My children whom I will send to you for help, thereby finding your-

self an integral part of the Great Brotherhood in the Kingdom of My Consciousness,
which I am establishing on earth even as it
is in Heaven.

THE ENEMY

MAN from the earliest day, even during his sojourn in Eden, has been aware of two forces within himself ever opposing each other,—one that would inspire and lead him to the highest, and the other to the lowest of thoughts, feelings and actions.

During his racial childhood man named that which called forth the lower phases of his nature the Devil, and thought of it as a malevolent power ever seeking to frustrate and keep from him the fulfillment of his desires. Later he questioned if it were not God punishing him for sins committed by with-holding from him the good things of life. But not until man grew up and his Real Self began to direct his thoughts was he able to see that what was holding him back and forcing him to be content with present if inadequate, possessions was but his own weakness of character and intellect, and that not until he had earned them could the powers unfold that came with knowledge and understanding, and could be exercised and controlled by him in the high use for which alone he began to see they were permitted and intended.

And with this knowledge gradually came the realization that these higher powers could not unfold while selfishness ruled him, and that selfishness was in some definite way related to the Devil of earlier days. It was then that man began to respond consciously to the leadings of his Higher Self, and to try to control and overcome selfishness. In so doing he found that when he yielded to the voice of self, trouble, failure, inharmony or suffering always resulted, and although he knew this and sought to avoid such, yet there was something within him that was stronger and made him yield to that hidden and persistent selfishness ever seeking to maintain complete control.

Thus he became aware that his greatest enemy was not some other person whom perhaps he had harmed or defrauded by such selfishness, but was that something within which was akin to the lowest phase of his own nature. When he listened to the voice of selfishness and not to that of his Higher Self—My Voice—it always brought harm, in that it made him suffer until his higher nature could again come into evidence, and could enable him to hear My Voice within, pointing out the sin he had committed againt his brother, and the necessity of repentance.

And then he gradually became conscious that when he considered committing any selfish act voices encouraging such act and suggesting ways and means poured into his mind from without, indicating he was being influenced by outside forces, thoughts from other minds, that were ever ready to push him on to his and others' undoing— if he listened and yielded to them.

Thus far man has come, learning that the *cause* of evil is in himself, in that weakness or lack of character which usually has selfishness at its root; but he had yet to learn that the *source* of evil is really without himself. For evil is not in Me, Whose mind is the only mind in man, but is inspired by the passions and thoughts sent forth by the forces of darkness, and which are ever seeking openings in self-separated human minds where selfishness, which is of their darkened

nature, is allowed to rule unchecked. Evil
hates Truth as darkness hates light, and
cannot exist where light is. Evil cannot
manifest and thrive in the light of Truth,
hence it must seek its own in order to live;
and selfishness exists only because of the
darkened sense of separation from Me, inspired by the enemy of light. When man
knows I am the only self of him, and that
it is My Mind, My Intelligence, My Will
and My Love that lives in and grows his
body and character and directs his life, and
he is willing to let Me rule, he has found
Truth, and that it is Truth that is making
him free from the power of self, even as
darkness always must disappear when the
light comes.

It is this fact that proves that the Enemy
can find entrance into man's mind only
when self in any way or at any time is al-

lowed to control, even if for but a short time. Once admitted and his subtle suggestions listened to, he is almost impossible to drive out until he has accomplished his will. For the selfishness that attracted him gave him his cue, and he is able to instill his poisonous idea to such effect, by feeding and encouraging the selfish desires and passions found there, that the mind becomes wholly blinded to Truth, and seeks thereafter only to satisfy the clamorings of self.

And the Enemy, who—what is he? Only the entitized form of the mass selfishness of men, that vast cumulation of the evil thoughts and passions of men's lower nature appropriated by Masters of Evil, grown great and powerful by their stealing and feeding off of the vital forces that their unsuspecting dupes at their instigation had poured into such evil thoughts and desires, thus giving them direct power over men through men's own life-force now absorbed and incorporated into their Master-nature, which they could thereby easily use to bend men to their will.

Do such Masters of Evil really exist? Yes, just as surely as evil men exist. These evil men are merely their servants, their dupes, their slaves, practically all unconscious of their Masters or of any outside power controlling them. In fact, all would deny and wholly refuse to believe in the existence of such Masters, so subtly have these Masters worked upon and deceived the thinking minds of men by instilling into them wrong beliefs about a personal God and an abstract devil, thus twisting their understanding of the inner laws of being so they would listen to and follow the prompting of their Masters who could then continue to control and exploit them to the accomplishment of their foul ends.

But, you ask, are these Masters of Evil living men, or do they exist only on the inner planes of being, like the Masters of Good?

If you can conceive of Masters of Good, then you may know also of these Masters of Evil, for if the former exist, so do the latter; and as there is a Christ who rules and leads and inspires the former, so is there an Anti-Christ who rules and leads and inspires the latter.

As the Christ can work on earth only through His disciples, who through love of their fellow men have emptied themselves of self so that their higher nature is ever waiting upon and serving Him; so the Anti-Christ can work only through his disciples who through hatred, jealousy, greed, and a continual exploiting of their fellows have grown so big and fat from self-indulgence and in their feeling of superiority that their lower nature has become a perfect instrument for the use of the great Exemplar of Selfishness.

Also as it is true that there are such Masters of both Good and Evil working on the Inner Planes of being and ever inspiring their disciples, so it is equally true that both these Masters are working also on the physical plane, living in human bodies, and doing the will of their respective Chiefs who abide on the Inner Planes.

Likewise do only those who have earned the right, by "living the life" of their respective Chiefs, the Christ or the Anti-Christ, ever come into personal contact with the Masters under whom they serve; for the Masters always remain in the background, and work through their disciples and agents, whom they have raised to places of influence and power because of their faithfully doing their Master's will. Those working consciously or unconsciously under Masters of Evil are always inspired and influenced towards Evil, while those under the banner of the Christ are inspired and led wholly to forget self and to work only for the uplifting of their fellow men.

All is according to the great Law—"As above, so below; as below, so above." Good and Evil are opposite poles, and therefore where one manifests there must also be the other to complement it and balance its power. But remember, both are but men's concept of an Infinite Reality, which changes not and cannot be affected by whatever men think of it as Good or Evil.

However, there are only a comparatively few of both so-called Good and Evil Masters working in human bodies at the present time, conscious of their Master degree, although many are preparing to enter human existence as soon as perfect conditions can be found. The Good Masters, under divine Law, will enter naturally into newly born infant bodies, and will over-shadow others —their disciples, while the Evil Masters, where opportunity offers, will deliberately break the Divine Law by dislodging and driving out the Souls of infants, thus stealing their bodies from them, or by driving out Souls from mature bodies, dispossessing them, and thereafter obsessing and impersonating such Souls to their friends and associates. Such in the near future will be of common occurrence, and will be made easy for them by all who succumb to fits of passion, indulgence in intense hatred, jealousy, or self-pity, or continual brooding over wrongs done them, or habitual condemnations of others, and who will suddenly wake one day in another world minus their physical bodies.

And be it known the Anti-Christ is also preparing to manifest himself, when all is ready and enough of such evil forces to serve his purpose are let loose on the earth and require his direction and control. For he has been preparing for this for thousands of years, training his Masters of Evil, who in turn have been carefully carrying out his plans with seldom any failure, through the agency of their earthly lieutenants — the great Bankers and Brokers of the money centers, the heads of Industrial Trusts, the Politicians, the Newspaper Editors, faithless Government Employees and Public Servants, any and all soulless individuals who seek only for self, and who unhesitatingly strike down ruthlessly those who stand in their way. These know not they are absolutely under the control of these forces of Evil; even if they knew, their moral fibre has become so weakened through habitual obedience to the selfish instinct fostered in them that they would have little power to resist the Master Forces ruling them. When the command goes forth, all these human agents will be compelled to fight under the banner of the Anti-Christ, him whom they have served so long, and who now claims and compels their absolute obedience.

But, you say, what of the Bankers, great Industrial Leaders, Editors, and the many thousands of other high-type minds who are involved in similar exploitations, and who are more or less unconscious of wrong-doing, because of having been brought up and trained in the so-called capitalistic consciousness? These cannot at present accept such unproved statements as the foregoing, and will naturally side with their associates on the enemy's side. What will become of them? Will they be condemned and destroyed with the Enemy, even though ignorant of evil-doing?

Do not be too sure of their ignorance, for there is that in every man which causes him to know when he is doing wrong—when he is taking advantage of a fellow man's ignorance, weakness or inability to prevent it, to benefit self.

While such do not realize the full extent of their crime against God, or know that they are actually serving the Great Enemy of man, yet the Truth is now being declared and is being broadcast over the earth, so that in time every man may hear. When the great tribulations that are shortly to fall upon mankind begin to manifest with ever-increasing and unmistakably vindictive violence, such men are going to think as they have never thought before, are going to desire to know Truth for itself with a mighty intensity, and are going to seek every possible way of escape. They will turn first to the churches, who will offer them a Christ crucified, who they say will save them. They will turn to Psychology, to Spiritualism, to the different cults, most of whom will offer them that favorite platitude the Enemy has been instilling into the minds of their followers during recent years—"There is no evil, there is only Good," when evil will be so everywhere about them that they can see, hear, feel, and therefore think of hardly anything else but evil. It is then that these seekers will be led by those Masters of Good, ever on the lookout to help every sincere searcher after Truth, to these declarations, and now they will be ready to listen to and recognize them as Truth. To all such who accept and now know whom they *were* serving, and who are willing and anxious to renounce forever self and all its claims,— to such will be shown not only the way of escape, but they will be lovingly led into a place of safety.

All this anticipates and at the same time announces to all who read to prepare for the great Battle of Armageddon shortly to begin on the physical plane, and which is already practically won on the Inner Planes, —for the Enemy with all his cohorts are being forced by the Powers of Good to the outermost of such realms, right up against the physical, where many think they can escape by thus stealing into human bodies.

But their existence there will be short-lived, for the battle will soon be waging with awful intensity in the outer, and the

mighty Forces fighting for righteousness
will quickly bring matters to such a crisis
that all the forces of darkness will be compelled to come out fully in the open so that
all people may see these forces and those
who fight with them, and forever after will
know them for the fiends they are.

And the battle, by the very fact of its being fought in the open, will be won by the
Forces of Light; for as darkness cannot exist
in the strong light of day, so with these
forces of evil (who draw all their life and
power from darkness, especially from the
darkened minds of men, purposely kept deceived and ignorant of their Divine Nature,
their Oneness with the Christ Mind), when
the Light of Divine Understanding is thus
poured into men's consciousness, they will
turn about, and because of the very destruc-
tiveness of their nature, will begin to destroy

each other, until none are left, and their souls will vanish into the chaos and darkness from which they came.

But think not this is not all in the Great Plan, and that the Anti-Christ and all his cohorts are not now wholly under My perfect control. For it is through him and his opposing forces that I provide the discipline and the punishment by which man learns to know unerringly Good *and* Evil. No man can truly know Good and Evil until he has tasted and eaten to satiation of the fruits of evil—has been so taught and led to the limit of selfish indulgence by the creator of evil —SELF, that he learns the foolishness and emptiness of it all, and finally awakens as a "Prodigal Son," and longs for his Father's house and the place at His table for goodness and abundance which he discarded for the husks of the outer world, and he starts on his homeward journey to his Father's Kingdom.

Those who have not awakened in this life to a knowledge of their spiritual nature must needs wait for a long, long period for another opportunity; for they cannot return to earth during the wondrous New Age I have prepared for My children who have listened to My Voice and whom I intend to lead into the Kingdom of Light and Love I am bringing down from Heaven into the midst of men.

THE KINGDOM OF HEAVEN

YOU have been told that the Kingdom of Heaven is within you, and many have accepted that statement as being so. But how many have ever purposely investigated and consistently endeavored to discover its real meaning,—how and where within, and how to find it?

It has been likened to many things by One Who unquestionably knew, Who was able to go in and out at will, from the powers He used, and which He ascribed not to Himself, but to His Father within the Kingdom which He said was within Himself.

It has been said elsewhere herein that the Kingdom is within the heart. But it cannot be within the physical heart is meant. What then is meant?

Even as the heart of anything is supposed to be the very center of that thing, so must it imply in the statement that the Kingdom is within man's heart; it must mean that it is deep within, at the very center of his being. And, of course, it cannot mean his physical being, but something much deeper within.

The only avenue of ingress to man's interior being must be through his mind, and most of those who have given any real thought to the subject have dimly perceived that the Kingdom of Heaven must be a state of consciousness within the mind. While it is indeed a state of consciousness, yet it is in very truth a place within the mind that can be reached by going there in consciousness, just as definitely and surely as you can go within your house, through several rooms, to an inner chamber in the very center, and there find your den or library, where you love to hide yourself from the world and find therein the privacy and quiet for study and work.

Let us imagine a house that is circular and very large, a house of many windows and doors. In this house the rooms are naturally in tiers, *i. e.,* there is an outer tier into which one enters through doors from the outside. Then there is a second tier connecting with the outer, and connecting with it a third tier surrounding one small room in the center.

Now let us consider this house as the human self, or that part of you that houses your personal or self-consciousness, that consciousness concerned with your physical body and its sensations, your emotions, feelings and desires, and all your thoughts, beliefs and opinions about yourself. While that part of your consciousness concerned with the realms outside of yourself, in which dwell all your concepts of things, conditions and other people, let us consider as your world, the world of physical or material things. Of course each has a different world from everyone else, for each has different concepts of those things which surround him and engage his interest; some things interest one that another never sees, and therefore such have no place in the other's world.

If we consider this house as comprising your self-consciousness, then the different rooms must be different states of your self-consciousness. Those in the outer tier must of course be what is termed the physical consciousness. There are five doors which connect it with the outer world of consciousness, called the doors of seeing, hearing, feeling, tasting and smelling. Through these doors all sense of the physical world without comes to you.

Suppose we then consider the next tier as that realm of consciousness within you that houses your desires, emotions and passions, from the lowest to the highest of such, called by some the astral realm and by others the desire world. You have read definite statements, made by those who have made a study of such states of consciousness, that these comprise an actual world within the mind, inhabited by the astral or desire bodies of all things that have physical bodies,—mineral, vegetable, animal or human, and also of some things above and below these kingdoms which naturally do not have physical bodies. And it is reasonable to accept that every world must have in it bodies composed of the natural substance of that world.

Likewise, let us suppose the next inner tier with its many smaller rooms to represent the mental realm of consciousness, which houses all your thoughts, concepts and ideas of whatever nature.

However, to make our analogy in perfect agreement with the statements above, within each of the three large tiers representing the physical, astral and mental realms there are seven smaller tiers or rows of rooms dividing and grading each realm of consciousness, from the lowest to the highest, and all so arranged that the highest of the physical row of that realm connects by special passageways with the highest row of the astral realm and then with the highest row of the mental realm; and likewise with each of the six other grades down to the lowest, the lowest being the outermost of each large tier or realm and the highest the innermost.

But also remember we are trying to depict here in the form of a circular house what properly should be shown as a spherical one, and that we are dealing with and entering into a fourth dimension of consciousness which cannot truly be described in terms of three dimensions. Even as Jesus tried to tell His disciples about the Kingdom, and had to use many parables that their human minds might be "lifted up" to glimpse this great state, so will it be necessary to read with other than mere brain intelligence to grasp the meaning behind the words herein used and the pictures they create.

We have tried, by going thus within the

mind, to picture the various states and realms of consciousness encountered in your journey to the center of your being. You know of the physical, emotional and mental realms within you, but you have not as yet penetrated the inner chamber, the den, the sanctuary, where the Master of the house dwells. This chamber can be entered only through one door which is always kept closed and opens only at the command of the Master himself.

Let us consider this inner chamber to be the sanctuary of the Soul, of the Real You, who are the Master of the house, into which none of the sensations, emotions, desires and thoughts of the outer realms are ever permitted to enter. But the Master, because of the peculiar, transparent nature of the walls (for they are only fancied walls, built out of the human sense of a separate mind), separating the different tiers or realms, can always look through them and see clearly all that is going on, and therefore is fully acquainted with everything present in the different rooms at all times. Likewise he naturally can go in and out of the different rooms at will, by simply entering into their consciousness, when of course he is immediately there.

The house, remember, we have pictured to represent the personality, or that combined consciousness concerned with the various, emotions and thoughts relating to the separate self, and which are housed in the different rooms (states of consciousness) of the different tiers (realms or worlds of consciousness) forming what you think is your separate mind. Also, remember, your world existing seemingly without your house of self you are conscious of in this same mind, proving that all you are and see and know exists only in your consciousness, and nowhere else.

Now try to realize this house of self was built by you in the long aeons past, when you first started on your outward journey from your Fathers House in the Garden of Eden (which House and Garden symbolize His Consciousness, even as the above house and the outer world symbolize your consciousness), and when you first began to think yourself separate in consciousness from Him. This thought of separation became a concept in your mind which in time, along with all your other thoughts of self, formed themselves around the center of your consciousness into what became your mental body; and later as this sense of separation became more real to you there grew about you what seemed to be realm after realm (tier after tier) of consciousness, forming what became your mental world.

Later you similarly built in consciousness around your mental body a desire or astral body, composed of all the desires, emotions, feelings, passions, fears, loves and hates of those early stages of tasting the experience of earning your bread by the sweat of your face, and with it formed in consciousness around you your astral world, containing similar desires and emotions from other centers of consciousness.

Then later, as these and many more fully developed thoughts and desires became established in your consciousness, they gradually crystalized there and seemed each to have solid and separate forms, thus bringing into being your concepts of physical or material bodies, and of the physical world in which they seemed to live and move and have their being.

But remember, all these various bodies, mental, astral, and physical, as well as the worlds in which they seemingly manifested, were but concepts existing only in that self-consciousness of your mind, which, by thinking yourself as separate from the Father Consciousness, now conceived every other thing also as in separate forms or pictures within itself, and which when impulsed by desire outmanifested themselves in astral matter, and later sometimes in physical matter.

Now try to realize that I, the God of you, am the Master within the little inner chamber of your house; that the house is part of My Mind even as is the little inner chamber. While what at present you think to be *You* is the combined consciousness of all the rooms or states in all the different realms or tiers within the house—outside of and surrounding the inner chamber, which as yet you are unable to enter; for remember, all the ideas, thoughts and concepts inhabiting those rooms compose the different states of consciousness you have built up since you separated yourself from Me long aeons ago. Therefore you must be what we can call the human part of *My* mind, that part which still *thinks* itself separate from Me. For as mind thinks so does mind become.

But know, *I alone AM*. The house of your mind must be and is a part of a center of My Mind, even as the different thoughts concepts, desires and emotions of the various rooms or states within your consciousness are parts or centers of *your* mind and consciousness. If your mind is a part of My Mind and you, therefore, are a center of my

Consciousness, then you *cannot* be separate from Me, but should be able to participate in that Consciousness of which *you are a part* and become one with Me. For I would open the door that you may walk in and sup with Me, and that all that I am you may also be, and all that I have may be yours for the taking. You are in My Consciousness—are a part of My Consciousness; therefore there can be no separation and you may *know* that You and I are ONE, always were One and always will be One. *Think* on these things and KNOW the Truth.

Now I will tell you a secret, which is only for those who have come with us thus far, —the inner chamber is a magical place; it is the *entrance* into the Kingdom you have been told to seek, for in very truth it is the door that admits you into My Consciousness. And once within you will learn that chamber which seemed small from the out- side in reality extends infinitely within, through realm after realm after realm with untold wonders and glories unfolding them- selves at every step. For in here you are no longer separate but are consciously one with Me, and My Consciousness is yours and all that it contains is also yours.

And here you learn another secret,—all that was without, in your seeming separate consciousness, were but reflections, sadly distorted reflections, darkened and mis- formed by ignorance, of the glorious reali- ties within, the realities your Soul had for so long been trying to lead you to, but which you insisted in looking for without in the world of things. For even as you look up in the heavens in the dark of night in the outer world and get glimpses of myriads of worlds and universes shining there, you can now understand they are but glimmering reflections trying to shine through the darkened human mind of the many beautiful mansions in the Kingdom of My Consciousness, awaiting those of My children who truly seek Me and who let My Word rule in their consciousness until it leads them to Me.

You ask, how may you seek within you and find that inner chamber that admits into the Kingdom of such a Heaven? By going *in imagination,* persistently, day after day, within your mind, through the different realms pictured above, seeking Me and Me only; by *visioning* yourself in the inner chamber as the Real You, your Highest Self,—as ME, the God of you; by thinking, speaking and acting as you imagine I think and speak and act,—until the very might of your desire and efforts at realization *com-*

pels Me to open the door and thereby to admit you into that Consciousness and that Home which was yours from the beginning.

For long, very long, have I been waiting for such a desire to manifest on your part, and that is why I keep the door closed and open it only in response to such an effort to find me. Think you I do not always know both your outer and your innermost thoughts, and cannot see you no matter where you are in consciousness? Remember the walls of self do not exist to Me, and I can look right through into man's secret desires and can easily see what motives rule, and especially what prompts him to seek within the house of his inner self.

My child, there is only one motive that will ever enable you to penetrate deep enough into consciousness to find Me, and that motive is a desire, a yearning, to serve

Me, the Christ within you and within every man; and when that yearning has become *first* with you and is the one supreme motive of your life, then I not only see you coming but I watch eagerly and send forth My love to help and spur you on.

After a period of trying and testing, of leading you into some of the rooms in the second tier of your house of mind within the realm of Desire, called by some the Realm of Illusion, to see if self still rules and if you can be distracted by the allurements of the astral senses; then if these do not hold you, leading you into the mental realms, named by some of the Hall of Learning, to see if intellect can entice you from your search by tempting you with the marvelous knowledge to be gained there; and if these do not stop you, then I am able to show forth from the Kingdom in your heart some of My real Nature, and may be able to open it wide enough to pour forth some of My Divine Love. And when that happens you begin to *feel* Me there, but not so that you know it is I—at first; you only feel My Love trying to find outlet, by leading you to others that I may help and bless them through you; and when others are brought to you, you feel it as a great longing to help them.

Thus do I gradually draw you in consciousness to the center of your being. And there sooner or later do you find the inner chamber—that it is your heart; and you now know you have a heart, and that it is in very truth the most wonderful and most important part of you; for from it issue all the vital things of life—and that most vital one of all, the power to help others.

And then suddenly one day you realize in

a great flash of illumination *what Love is*—
that Love is God, and that what you feel in
your heart is His Presence there. You then
know that Love which issues from the heart
is God's life, is *your* life, that His life and
your life cannot be separate, but that
through your consciousness of God's Love in
your heart, you are He, and He is you—*you*
are ONE!

And then, as you learn consciously to
open your heart and let Love out, you find
it is a magical, a wonderfully brilliant Light
that shines through and radiates from you,
clearing away all mists and shadows from
your human mind, enabling you to see with
My eyes and to know with My understanding all things I desire you to know.

And as it thus radiates from you it ever
goes before you and penetrates to the soul
of those who come to you, quickening like-

wise their hearts so that the words I speak through you find lodgment in their minds, and awaken them and make them aware of Me in *their* hearts, through the response they feel there to the Love coming from you. And they too are thus given a glimpse of the Kingdom within, proving that I, the Christ, am the Light that lighteth every man that cometh into the world—when I am able, through a human channel, thus to pour My Love into the heart of man, and light the wick that I have previously prepared there.

I have now shown you the way into the Kingdom, that it is through the door of the heart into the little chamber within; that only Loving Service will open the door and admit you and enable you to go in and out at will.

I will not tell you now about the won-

drous life within the Kingdom, except to
say that Love is the one and only life there,
the life that all who abide there breathe,
absorb, feed upon, grow with and build from
strong, beautiful Souls. Love in very truth is
the vitalizing, energizing Force animating,
inspiring and directing all activities there;
all there abide continually in My Consciousness, receiving freely of all that I am and
have; and there even as here with you, as
they let Love rule and fill their whole being, am I enabled to serve the more through
them on all planes and in all realms of My
Consciousness.

Many there are in the world today who
in the past have found the Kingdom and
who are here now to help Me awaken the
many thousands more who are longing and
yearning to be shown the way unto Me.
They are the ones whom I have sent to an-

swer the call of those who have asked, who have sought, who have knocked; for have I not promised that those who ask *shall* receive, and those who seek *shall* find, and those that knock it *shall* be opened unto them?

But I can only serve My earth children through channels I have prepared, through those who have become empty of self and who now live only to serve. They are of the Kingdom on High, that Great Brotherhood of the Spirit, who are here and are actually bringing Heaven down to earth into the consciousness of many men these days. They are My blessed ones, the forerunners of that Brotherhood which soon is going to manifest, to live, work and rule on the earth, and which is going to raise it to the Heaven, that they two no longer may be separate but may appear as One to all men, as they are in the Great Reality.